The
Ghastly Greek
GODS

*Classical Mythology You'll Actually
WANT to Read!*

T R Winters

Order this book online at www.trafford.com
or email orders@trafford.com

Most Trafford titles are also available at major online book retailers.

Printed in the United States of America.

ISBN: 978-1-4907-1962-7 (sc)
ISBN: 978-1-4907-1963-4 (e)

Trafford rev. 12/10/2013

 www.trafford.com

North America & international
toll-free: 1 888 232 4444 (USA & Canada)
fax: 812 355 4082

Contents

Dedicated with much
love and admiration to
Mum
and
Sarah Trickett,
the two most influential
women in my life.

Introduction

A long time ago a lot of gods lived in Ancient Greece. I have no idea why they all lived there, but they did. Maybe they liked the climate.

In any case it's a jolly good thing for us that they did live there, because they weren't very nice gods. In fact they were ghastly.

They lived on a fancy, invisible elevated platform that sort of floated over Greece. It's a real pity they didn't just stay up there because when they came down HERE, they were a right pest.

In fact, if they turned up in our world today, we'd probably be obliged to set traps for them and once they were caught to chuck them in jail. After all, we no longer consider it all right to start the day on a hearty breakfast of roast toddler, wander out to indulge in a wee bit of murder and round out the afternoon with a spot of cheating.

If you think the police force is overworked as it is, just imagine the state we'd be in if those ghastlies ever resurrected.

But fortunately for us the immortals all died off, and left us safe and sound with our delightfully enlightened society where it is illegal for a mother to broil her son.

But just because the ghastlies all died doesn't mean their ghosts don't still haunt us. And sometimes a ghost can be even more dangerous than the original being.

So if on your journey through life you ever encounter a ghastly ghost, I hope you remember the original ghastly god and use your wits to defeat it.

Kindest Regards, Tiffany R Winter.

hapter One

A Very Ghastly God and his Diabolical Dad

"This is Tacticus Atticus with Ancient World News. Today we have a very special guest. Ladies and gentlemen, please give a warm welcome to Rhea, a direct descendant of Gaia, mother of the earth."

Sound of applause and cheering.

"Rhea has had a fascinating career. Born into the Titan dynasty, she was given in marriage to her brother Kronos, and bore him six children, five of which Kronos devoured.

Her youngest child was of course, the illustrious Zeus, and that's what we are here to talk about."

Cheering from the audience. A few people are waving cards saying "Go Rhea!" and "We love you Zeusey!"

"Great to have you here Rhea!"

"Yeah, it's good I could find the time to be here."

"So, I think if I look at your life, the word that comes to mind is, well, overcomer. I mean, you had an arranged marriage to your BROTHER,"

sounds of groans and vomiting from the audience,

"and on top of that, he ate your children. So I guess what we all want to know is, how did you raise a supreme god?"

"Well you know Tacticus, it wasn't easy. But when Zeus was born I decided that one of my children was not going to spend his life in my husband's stomach."

"Hmm, so you made a difficult decision didn't you?"

Rhea dabs her eyes slightly.

"Yes Tacticus I did. I, I . . . . oh excuse me, it's . . . . Oh, I'm sorry . . . ."

"Hmm, the hurt is still there isn't it Rhea?"

"Yeah it really is. I decided that I couldn't raise this child. His father would just eat him. So I gave my baby boy to his Grandmother and some nymphs to raise."

Gasps of sympathy from the audience.

"And how did this make you feel about Kronos?"

"Honestly? I hated him. I just hated him . . . ."

"What happened to Zeus?"

"Well, my mother-in-law, who was also my mother, raised him among the shepherds of Mt Ida. That was bad for Zeus, he always had horrible hygiene . . . . he stunk."

"Oh my, I never thought of that before . . . ."

"Most don't. But after a while he started to ask questions about who he was, and where he came from."

"And did he have any rejection issues about you leaving him?"

"Not really, but he was upset that his father had tried to eat him."

"Really?"

"Yeah, he was quite cross about it. He created a poison to kill Kronos."

"How did you feel about this?"

"I sent him the recipe."

"Did it work?"

"Sort of, Kronos got very sick. Then he started vomiting and passing gas. It was really gross. Eventually he threw up all my other children."

"Hestia, Demeter, Hera, Hades and Poseidon?"

"That's right. You know, Zeus wasn't happy that his father had tried to eat him, but the kids that Kronos had managed to eat . . . ."

"They were angry?"

"They were livid. They hated his guts, and believe me, they knew all about his guts."

"This is where Zeus emerges as a leader isn't it?"

"Yeah, he gave a beautiful speech, it brought tears to my eyes, he said 'Kronos is a rat bag, a scoundrel and a cannibal. Let's get him!'"

"And did they 'get' him?"

"Well, they tried. But after ten years of warfare the outcome was still in the balance, so Zeus decided to take extreme action."

"Yes, he released the children of earth didn't he?"

"Yes, that's right, the dastardly Cyclops. It was a risk, the Cyclops are an unpredictable people, but the only thing Zeus ever really wanted in life was unlimited power. I mean, it was his dream, and sometimes you have to take risks to pursue your dreams . . . ."

"That is so profound! And what was the outcome of this risk?"

"Oh it was magical! The Cyclops were so grateful to Zeus and his siblings that they gave them all the loveliest presents. Zeusie got a nice loud and destructive pair of thunderbolts, Poseidon got a gorgeous trident (so useful for stabbing people) and Hades got a spooky helmet of darkness!"

"And these gifts were helpful?"

"Heck yeah, they were invincible. And that's when I got the shock of my life . . . ."

"Awww, you were reunited with your boy?"

"NO! Zeus rounded us all up, and threw us into outer darkness!"

"WHAT?!"

"I was so angry, I was screaming at him, 'you twerp! I should have let your father eat you!'"

"Wow, I did not see that coming! What did he say to you?"

"'Whatever Mum, talk to the hand . . . .'"

"Oh my goodness! And that's how he became the supreme god?"

"No, my mother and Mother-in-law, Gaia, was furious."

"Really, what did she say to him?"

"$#@*&^%$$%^#@$#%$&%*^*&%*&*&#% ^&^&*(&(&*!!!!!!!!!!!!!!!!!"

"Umm, oh dear. Did she do anything else?"

"She sent the giants and Typhon against him."

"Who is Typhon?"

"Oh, a chap we used to call Unbeatable Bert. He has these huge wings and enormous teeth."

"What happened?"

"We changed his name."

"Really? To what?"

"Beaten Bert."

"So Zeus won?"

"Yeah he did. And I know it's strange, 'cause to this day he won't acknowledge me, and he pays Hades to say mean things to me, but I can't help it, I'm just so proud of that boy!"

"Err, OK."

"I mean how many mothers can say their sons became supreme gods? I mean, he goes around zapping people with thunder and burning them to cinders and even the other gods are scared of him."

"So you like that?"

"Oh definitely, Zeus always wanted power. You know, he always wanted to be able to do whatever he liked and get away with it. He worked hard for that, and I think we should respect that."

"Wow, what a story, so I guess what everyone is wondering, is . . . . oh excuse me, someone has just come on the stage. And who are you sir?"

"Hades. Hey Mum, you shouldn't be out here, Zeus wants you incarcerated for infinity. It's back to the underworld for you."

"Listen young man, I am not going back there!"

"Yeah Mum, you are."

"@$#@%@%#! I should have let your father eat Zeus! @^%$@^%$%#! And I should have let him digest you! Let go of my arm, you toad!"

"Come on Mum . . ."

"#%#@%$#%#$%!!!!!!"

They leave the stage, Hades glowering and Rhea using unprintable words.

"Well um, thank you for your time Rhea! And let that serve as a inspiration to the rest of you. Anything is possible if you are willing to work hard and kill for it."

"Thank you for watching 'Ancient World News', I'm your host Tacticus Atticus. Be sure to tune in next time for when we interview Media, ex-wife of Jason, captain of the Argo in 'Jason and the golden fleece, glorious hero or pathetic moron?'"

Theme Music.
Credits

Disclaimer.
'Ancient world news' takes no responsibility for any 'child gobbling' 'domestic violence' 'civil war' or 'general weirdness' that may result from the viewing of this programme.

hapter Two

Grubby Zeus Gets His Goddess

One day Zeus decided he wanted to get married. He already had a lot of girlfriends, but his house was a hovel and he was sick of living like a pig.

"Girlfriends are a lot of fun," he grumbled to himself, "but they are awfully unhelpful about picking up after me." He scratched his chin thoughtfully. "But I certainly don't want to pay a housekeeper. Zeus old boy, it looks like it's time to go steady and get yourself a wife."

He looked at his palace. It wasn't an encouraging sight. It was crammed full of dirty laundry and unwashed dishes.

"Yuck," said Zeus, "the sooner the better I reckon, then I shall be able to throw my clothes all over the place and my wife shall pick them all up for me."

After a lot of careful consideration, because after all the choosing of a wife is a serious business, Zeus decided that the most suitable woman for him was a goddess called Hera.

"Such a tidy woman," thought Zeus approvingly, glancing round his piggy palace. "That's the girl for me, she should get this place whipped into shape in no time!"

So off to court Hera went Zeus.

Hera was busily sweeping her porch when Zeus slouched up.

"Well hello, Beautiful," boomed Zeus, waggling his eyebrows in smug anticipation of his impending marriage.

Hera glanced coldly at Zeus's grubby tunic and filthy face.

"What do you want?" she snapped.

"I want you to marry me," announced Zeus importantly. "Won't that be a nice treat for you Hera?"

"NO, it would NOT be nice," snarled Hera. "Everyone knows what a dirty little sleazebag you are, Zeus."

Zeus scowled. "There's no need to exaggerate, Hera!" he shouted.

"No there isn't," Hera agreed heartily. "Your womanizing is quite bad enough without embellishment!"

Zeus didn't know what 'embellishment' meant, but he realised with a shock that he had found a woman who was impervious to his waggling eyebrows. And this simultaneously infuriated and delighted him.

"Oh yeah!?" shrieked Zeus. "Well I say you're gonna fall for me, Hera!"

"And I say if you don't get your dirty filthy person off my porch you're going to fall onto the ground!" snarled Hera.

"Really? Why?" asked Zeus unwisely.

"Because I'm going to shove you there!" roared Hera, running at him with her broom.

WHACK! WHACK! WHACK! WHACK!

Zeus tumbled off the porch and fell smack onto the ground. Hera pushed her clean, stern face into his. "NOTHING would induce me to marry a licentious little toad like YOU!" she shouted. "And if you know what's good for your health, you WILL NEVER MENTION IT AGAIN!"

Hera whirled around and stormed into her immaculate home.

Zeus sat up and rubbed his head. "WOW!" said Zeus, "I simply must have that woman!"

And Zeus proceeded to make a huge nuisance of himself at Hera's.

He sat on her porch and sang beastly, sappy love songs in a flat, tuneless drone. He smelt so bad he brought the flies and Hera was obliged to invest in a fly swat.

He prowled around her kitchen in hopes she would reward him with a piece of cake and received instead a smack with a rolling pin.

He stationed himself outside her parlour window and yelled endearments through the lattice.

"Hey darling! I bet you're jolly good at darning socks eh!?"

"GO AWAY!"

"I've got a whole pile of socks Sweetheart. If you marry me, I'll let you darn every single one!"

"GO KICK A BUCKET!"

"I love you!"

"OH YEAH?! WELL, I HATE YOU!"

This went on for years. If Hera lived nowadays she would have taken out a protection order against Zeus, but back then all she could do was ignore him and hope he would go away.

It didn't work.

One day while Hera was hurrying home with a basket of shopping Zeus popped out of the hedge. He was accompanied by his colony of flies and a nasty smell.

"How about a cuddle, Hera!" he boomed, flinging his dirty arms wide open.

Hera stopped and glared at him. "Zeus," she said, "the day I give you a cuddle is the day I will marry you!"

"Really?" gasped Zeus incredulously.

"It'll never happen," said Hera tartly.

But Zeus wasn't used to being thwarted forever and foolish Hera had given him a cunning plan.

Early the next morning Zeus climbed up to the top of Mount Thornax. It was one of Hera's favourite picnic spots.

Zeus was a god and thus had quite a bit of magical ability. He mumbled a few magic words to himself and 'Poof' he transformed himself from a smelly god into a shivering cuckoo bird.

Really, it was a huge improvement.

"He he!" sniggered the cuckoo bird, "I'm a genius! I'm finally gonna get me a wife to pick up after me!"

He balanced on a tree branch and began to shiver theatrically.

Along came Hera.

"Br-r-r-r-r-r-r-r-r-r-r!" chattered the cuckoo.

Hera didn't hear him.

The cuckoo hopped closer. **"BR-r-r-r-r!"** He shivered as loudly as he could.

Nothing. Hera was still enjoying the view.

"What a horribly selfish woman," sniffed the cuckoo, "ignoring a poor, helpless little bird!"

"BR-r-r-r-r-r-r!!!!!" roared the infuriated cuckoo.

Hera looked around vaguely before she returned to her picnic.

"Bah!" thought the cuckoo. "What an egomaniac! what a narcissistic cat!" And he flung himself to the ground in front of her.

"OH!" cried Hera. "You poor dear thing!"

"Ah ha," thought the cuckoo excitedly, "here we go!"

Hera tenderly lifted the cuckoo from the ground and cuddled it to warm it.

"AH HA HA HA HA HA HA HA HA HA HA HA !"

Zeus discarded his cuckoo body and flung his great big dirty arms around Hera. "Waa ha ha ha ha ha!" gloated Zeus. "I got my cuddle and now you have to marry me, Hera!"

"Ugh!" screamed Hera. "Get away from me you horrid lizard! How dare you touch me, you reptile!"

"Oh ha ha!" giggled Zeus. "It's perfectly appropriate for a man to cuddle his fiancée!"

"I shall never marry you!" screamed Hera, struggling against him.

"Bit late for that kind of talk!" cackled the ex-cuckoo, picking Hera up and slinging her over his shoulder. "Come on sweet one, time to visit the marriage celebrant!"

So Zeus married Hera. Then they went off on their honeymoon. Being deities you could hardly expect them to settle for the standard two weeks, but honestly, three hundred years does seem a touch excessive.

It probably took Zeus that long to convince Hera that she was his wife and annulment wasn't an option.

After this elongated vacation, Zeus returned to Mount Olympus to resume his duties as the CEO of the ghastlies.

And Hera discovered why Zeus had really married her.

Just imagine what would happen if YOU trashed your bedroom and left it alone for three hundred years.

It was like entering a landfill. There were a few bats mouldering around and as for cobwebs! There were so many cobwebs you could have used them as insulation.

"Aaaaah!" shrieked Hera. "What a pigsty!"

"Yup," said Zeus, looking happily from the filth to his capable, tidy wife. "And you get to clean it all up. Hee hee!"

"Pardon me?" said Hera in a dangerous voice.

Zeus pulled his socks off and threw them on the floor. "You can start by picking those up!" he told her bossily.

Hera glared at Zeus. "I have a horrible feeling about this marriage!" she said sternly. "I have the distinct impression that you think you're got a free housekeeper."

"Yup," agreed Zeus, spitting cheerfully into the sink.

"WELL YOU HAVEN'T!" screamed Hera in rage, "DO YOU REALLY THINK YOU GET TO BOSS ME AROUND JUST BECAUSE YOU'RE THE MAN?!"

"Yup!" beamed Zeus. "Good idea eh?!"

This was not a wise thing for Zeus to say. Hera started to throw things at him and I regret to tell you that for all his godliness, Zeus had no inhibitions about throwing things at his wife.

They fought all the time.

Hera would scream and yell at Zeus and Zeus would smack her in the nose.

After a while Zeus had a baby. Just how Zeus managed to have the baby is very confusing, but then, there were many confusing aspects to the ghastlies.

It was a girl and they called her Athena. Athena was rather clever. She was a book worm who studied enormous piles of scrolls on military history and strategy. She was good looking but she disliked pretty clothes and she liked to clank around in a humongous suit of armour.

They also had Ares. They decided to be a touch more traditional this time and Hera carried the baby to term.

Ares shared his sister's devotion to war, but where Athena was a theorist, Ares was a terrorist and liked to apply what he had learnt.

"Where have you been Ares?" shouted Hera when he arrived home late one night, well past his curfew.

"I've had a bonza time Mum!" yelled Ares, waving a bloodied sword around and grinning a nasty grin. "First I started a war that didn't need to be started, then I fought on one side and when I'd killed loads of people for THAT side, I switched sides and killed the OTHER side! Waa ha ha ha ha ha ha! By golly it was fantastic!"

Zeus smirked with pride. "Dear boy," he chortled, "I'm so proud of you!"

"By crickey mate!" boomed Ares, "I just love war! It's just so much fun! And it's so blimmin good for the economy!"

Poor Hera. Some women cope with abusive marriages by being extremely grateful for their children, but Athena and Ares were such a horrible pair even that avenue of comfort was closed.

They had a couple more children, but they don't really count. When Hephaestus was born as an ugly cripple, Hera threw him away.

When Hebe was born she was such beauty they decided to keep her around to serve them delicious beverages. But after a while Zeus spotted someone even better looking, so they threw Hebe away too.

In the end Hera gloomily adapted herself to her position as the Queen of Mount Olympus. It was an important occupation, and being a ghastly goddess she wasn't without that touch of haughty arrogance that marked the gods of old.

In fact, there were just a few times that Hera and Zeus teamed up. Generally, this was because they had discovered someone that they mutually hated, and they considered bullying a team effort.

"Zeus!" yelled Hera one day, "that ugly old Centaur, Ixion tried to kiss me today!"

"OH he did, did he!" roared Zeus. "Well, we'll jolly well see about that!"

Zeus created a Hera shaped cloud and popped it out in the street. When Ixion galloped up and tried to kiss the cloud, Hera and Zeus rushed out.

"Ah ha!" snarled Zeus, "You kissed my wife!"

"No I didn't," said poor old Ixion, looking confused. "I think I kissed a cloud. It was rather soggy."

"Yes!" yelled Zeus. "But it was a Hera shaped cloud!"

"Get him Zeus!" screamed Hera, jumping up and down in a fury. "Do something really awful!"

"I'm sorry!" wept the centaur. "It was wrong, I know! Please forgive me!"

"When I can have the fun of torturing you instead?" guffawed Zeus. "Not likely, mate!"

And He and Hera tied Ixion to a blistering hot chariot wheel and set it revolving around the universe for all eternity.

"I don't understand!" wept Ixion as he rolled out into the cosmos. "You have loads of affairs, Zeus, and nobody punishes you! Why do we have to be moral when our gods aren't?"

"Oh pooh, pooh!" snorted Zeus. "I'm god! I get to make the laws, but there's no way I'm going to obey them! That would make the law a more powerful ruler than ME!"

"Mercy!" sobbed Ixion, as his ears started to sizzle. "Forgive me!"

"Mercy!?" snarled Zeus. "Do I look like a COWARD to you!?" And he kicked the fiery wheel into a gallop.

"Ha ha!" shrieked Hera, as Ixion became a pretty little spot of gold in the sky. "You showed him, Zeus!"

"Oh yes I did!" sniggered Zeus conceitedly. "There's nothing more important or powerful than us gods in the whole world! We can do whatever we like and get away with it!"

And off they went to dinner, callously disregarding poor old Ixion, doomed to roam the universe forever without any hope of redemption.

Chapter Three

Hapless Hephaestus
Marries Awful Aphrodite

My name is Hephaestus. My mum was the goddess Hera and my dad was Zeus, the top god.

I suppose I should have been a prince, coming from that family, but I was born with crooked shoulders and a lame leg.

When I was born, Dad threw up. Then he said, "Oh yuck, what a monstrosity, fancy having to tell people that's my son."

Mum was very upset about this, naturally.

She said, "Don't talk like that, Zeus! Of course we aren't going to tell people he's our son! We'll just get rid of him."

WHAT!?

"Oh good idea, darling," said Dad.

PARDON ME!?

"But darling, how do we get rid of a kid? I mean, they come with a no refund policy."

YEAH THAT'S RIGHT DAD, I'M GLAD YOU REMEMBERED!

"Oh really, darling, use your imagination, just chuck him in the garbage disposal."

EXCUSE ME??????!!!!!!!!!!

But did anyone listen to me? No, I was just an ugly blotch on the beauty parade of their lives.

Dad threw me in the garbage disposal.

The last thing I heard as I was falling through the drain pipe was Mum and Dad sniggering about how big my nose was.

I don't want to complain about this, but being thrown in the garbage disposal as a baby can really give you rejection issues. I guess if your own parents reject you it's kind of hard to believe anyone will ever accept you.

I fell for a long time. Apparently my divine family consider the human world to be their septic tank because all the plumbing from Mount Olympus ends up there.

The garbage disposal drain comes out at an island in Greece called Limnos.

I was lying on the ground feeling really awful, I mean, most parents throw a party when they have a child, but mine had just thrown up.

Then a bunch of people called Sintians came along and rescued me. They took me home, gave me a dagger to chew on and raised me as a son.

Wow, can you believe that, these people actually cared about me.

Sure, they were pirates and the men provided for their families by murdering and looting other families, but AT LEAST THEY NEVER THREW ME IN A GARBAGE DISPOSAL!

When the Sintians weren't off having a jolly adventure killing and maiming people, they liked to work in their forges forging lovely big weapons of mass destruction.

Those Sintians just loved killing and when you are passionate about your job you have to have the right tools.

I worked right alongside them, making axes and crowbars and head-bashers. Ooh it was lovely fun.

Then I started experimenting with jewellery. Those Sintian men were too busy with war craft to worry about giving their wives any pleasure, but you know, women just love jewellery and well, since my own mum had booted me out, those women were all I had.

So I started making them necklaces and bracelets and they were so grateful.

After a while I started thinking about Mum and how ungrateful she was. How she hadn't even given me a chance. She'd judged me on my appearance, and because I wasn't good looking she threw me out.

I wondered what terrible circumstances had made her so harsh. What secret sorrow was she enduring?

The more I thought about the secret grief that she must surely be hiding, the more I wanted one thing—

REVENGE!

Yes, I wanted to destroy my mother just as she had destroyed me.

Nothing, and I mean NOTHING excuses a woman throwing her son into a garbage disposal.

So I devised a cunning trap. I went off to my forge and I crafted a beautiful chair for Dearest Mummy.

It was very beautiful and very dangerous.

I posted Mummy dearest her chair (Classical Couriers, they deliver to mortals and gods alike) and waited.

Ha ha I didn't have to wait long.

Mum loved her anonymous gift. She sat down in it and SNAP it grabbed her tight and wouldn't let go.

BWA HA HA HA HA HA HA HA HA HA HA HA HA!

Serves her jolly well right!

After a while Mum started to get hungry and then she got thirsty and it looked like Mummy dearest would soon be Mummy deadest.

Then the other gods at Mount Olympus got a bit worried. I guess they were afraid they might be next.

Somehow they tracked me down as the maker of the chair of chastisement and suddenly, wow, they wanted me back to let Mum go.

I thought about it, then I thought about the garbage disposal and I told them, "Forget it! The old hag deserves everything she's getting!"

For a bunch of deities they sure are dumb. They couldn't break the magic spell and set Mum free.

I was so happy. Every time I thought of Mum dying a horrible death I laughed and laughed.

Then a god came to visit me whom I'd never meet before. He was fat and jolly and he said his name was Dionysus.

I told him straight, "Look, if you want to talk about Mum, as far as I'm concerned, I have no mother."

Dionysus was so reasonable about it. He said "Hey man, I completely understand. I would never force my beliefs on you dude, and as long as you don't force your beliefs on me, we are so cool dude."

"I'm touched Dionysus," I said. "All the other gods keep telling me I'm a rat bag for trying to kill my mother."

"Dude, if you are OK with what you believe, then I am so happy for you. I just wanted to introduce you to this revolutionary new drink I invented. It's booze dude, so let's booze dude!"

So we boozed. And I got, well, to be perfectly honest, err, to not to put too fine a point on it, well, I GOT DRUNK OK?

Boozed, sozzled, stoned.

Look, everyone makes a mistake every now and then. BE COOL DUDES!

Dionysus took care of me. He called for a sober donkey and took me home to sleep off my night of fun.

When we got to his house all I wanted to do was go to bed. No, wait, first I wanted to throw up, and THEN go to bed.

But Dionysus wouldn't let me.

He dragged me into a room with a woman sitting in a chair. The woman looked very thin and very cross.

"Come on dude!" said Dionysus. "Let her go."

I tried to fall onto the floor, but Dionysus hauled me up. "Let her go dude!" he snarled.

"Be cool dude!" I slurred, but Dionysus didn't smile.

"Let, her, go!" he hissed.

So I let her go. It was easy. The chair had magic snaps on it like the one I made for Mum.

Then I threw up.

It's really just too bad I threw up on the woman. She didn't seem to like it very much.

In the morning when I woke up I realized Dionysus had tricked me and I'd let Mum go.

I was furious, naturally, and I decided to have it out with Dionysus.

I said, "You lowdown scum! You tricked me! You got me drunk and made me let Mum go!"

"Hey man," said Dionysus, "it's like I said, I won't force my opinions on you and you better not force your opinions on me. You think it's OK to kill your mother, I'm cool with that. I happen to think it's OK to deceive lame dumb dodos."

OUCH! That really hurt.

Anyway, here I was back in Mount Olympus. Dionysus told me that the other gods had taken up a kitty and clubbed together to buy me a palace of my own.

Despite being mad, I was kind of touched.

Oh boy, that didn't last long. It turns out that the 'palace' the gods had bought me was a giant forge.

A real hovel.

Mum told me, "Congratulations Ugly, you're the official metal worker around here now. So get cracking, we all want beautiful thrones."

Then she glared at me. "And they better not be TRICK thrones this time!"

Wow, just what I always wanted, slaving for a bunch of bossy gods.

After a while though, I noticed something. The gods might have been really nasty to work for, but some of those girl gods were really attractive.

I mean REALLY attractive.

There was this goddess called Athena. You talk about a looker!

I asked her out once.

She accepted and I assumed it was because she was so impressed that I had a real job unlike all the other lazy layabouts up in Mount Olympus.

To start with the date went really well. She was so beautiful, all I wanted to do was look at her.

Unfortunately she insisted on talking the whole time. It wasn't very nice talk. It was also very, very loud talk. The entire restaurant could hear her.

"What I love in life," she shouted, "is war."

I coughed politely. "Oh, um really?" I said.

"I just love watching a jolly good bloodbath!" she yelled, stabbing her fork into the table. "I love watching maiming and killing! By golly it's lovely fun!"

"Oh hum, interesting," I mumbled. "What do you enjoy studying?"

"Military strategy!" boomed Athena.

"Do you like cooking?" I asked hopefully.

"Boring!" shouted Athena. "Who wants to cook when they can be leading warriors into battle and bossing generals around?!"

"Laundry?"

"Yuck!"

Oh well, not every goddess is a domestic goddess and she was very pretty.

"How about marrying me, dear Athena?"

"Oh ha ha ha ha!"

"No, I mean it! I'll work at my forge and provide for you, darling. I won't force you to give up your career, and I'll make you so happy my pet."

"Get a life, weirdo, no one wants to marry a lame little dweeb!"

So much for that.

I went back to my forge and I cried and sulked for a bit and then I started on the mountain of orders the other gods had left me.

I was the son of Zeus, but as far as they were concerned, I was just a commodity of convenience. A divine vending machine, a worthless ugly cripple.

Then one day I got a letter from Dad. He wanted to see me.

I met him in his study.

"My boy!" he exclaimed, flinging his arms open.

I didn't leap into his arms. Last time I'd been in those arms, I had ended up in a garbage disposal.

"My precious son! Last time I saw you, you were so tiny." He sniffed.

"Yeah, you said I was too ugly to be your son."

"My boy, let us let bygones be bygones. I hear you long to marry!"

"I guess . . . ."

"And I have chosen a bride for you my son. Such a beauty, such a luscious peach!"

This sounded interesting.

"I've decided that only the best will do for my best boy. So I'm going to give you Miss Aphrodite as a wife."

My mouth fell open.

"But, Dad, isn't she a . . . ."

"Yes my boy, yes, she's a supermodel."

"Oh wow, Dad, THANKS!"

"Ha ha, that's quite all right my boy. Your wedding is tomorrow at ten o'clock. Be on time, don't keep your little sugarplum waiting!"

Well I floated out of there I can tell you! Fancy me, ME, Hephaestus the cripple marrying the goddess of love and beauty!

Talk about a happy ending.

That evening as I tidied up the forge for my princess I heard a knock on the door.

I opened it and there stood Ares. I don't really like Ares. He's the god of war and he's always looking for trouble.

"Gidday mate," he said in a nasty voice. "I hear you got yourself a shelia?"

I smirked. I couldn't help it. Here was Ares, the good looking bachelor, without a girlfriend, and me on the eve of my wedding to the most beautiful creature in the world.

"Yup," I said, "I got a shelia."

"I reckon you think that's bonza, mate?" snarled Ares.

I smirked again. "I reckon."

"Well *I* don't!" snarled Ares. "And do yah know *why* I don't think that's bonza, mate?"

"Not really."

"Because you've got MY sheila mate!" screamed Ares.

"Now now, Ares, that can hardly be true. Miss Aphrodite is marrying *me*. So she can hardly be your sheila can she?"

"Idiot! Zeus is forcing her to marry you so that she can't marry me! She thinks you are just a lame dingo with the brain of a wombat!"

Crikey. Talk about a way to ruin the night before your wedding.

The wedding wasn't much better. My bride was very beautiful. But she was wearing a pair of handcuffs and yelling rude words at all the guests.

Ares was one of the guests. As I took my wife's hand, he looked at me and slid his finger across his throat.

"Yer dead meat, mate!" he hissed.

Crumbs.

Being married to a supermodel wasn't nearly as much fun as I had thought it was going to be. Aphrodite spent the first three days of our honeymoon locked up in my bedroom making up obnoxious poems about me and yelling them through the keyhole.

I had to sleep on the cold floor.

On the fourth evening she emerged. She was wearing a beautiful dress and drenched in rosewater.

Things seemed to be looking up.

But then the doorbell rang.

I opened it and there stood Ares.

"How's it going mate?" he smirked. "Enjoying yah Shelia?"

I scowled at him.

"Oh Daaaaaaaaaaaaaarhling!" shrieked Aphrodite, shoving me out of the way and flinging herself into Ares's arms, "you remembered our date!"

"Too right shelia." said Ares, giving her (MY WIFE!) a big smack on the lips.

I picked myself up off the floor where my wife had thrown me.

"Aphrodite!" I said, a bit crossly, "are you going out on a date with Ares?"

"Of course I am!" shouted my wife, giving my face a whack, "it'll be more fun than staying around here with a lame dingo like you."

"With the mind of a wombat mate!" added Ares.

Then they started laughing at me.

"Bwa ha ha ha ha ha ha ha ha ha ha ha ha ha ha ha ha ha ha ha ha ha ha ha ha ha ha ha ha ha ha ha ha ha ha ha ha ha ha ha ha ha ha ha ha ha ha ha ha ha ha ha ha ha ha ha ha ha ha!"

So Ares and Aphrodite (MY WIFE!) went off on a date. That was Monday night.

On Tuesday night she went off on a date with Poseidon.

On Wednesday she went out with Hermes.

On Thursday she went out with Dionysus.

On Friday she went out with Adonis.

On Saturday she went out with Phaethon.

And on Sunday she went out on a date with Anchises.

It was all plain to me now. Dad hadn't given me a good wife at all. Oh, she was pretty all right. Pretty AWFUL that is.

But I didn't give up hope. I still thought I could make the marriage work.

One night while she was away (of on a date with Brutes) I got busy and made her a lavish gift. It was simply gorgeous.

A magic golden girdle that would make her even more lovely to look at. Aphrodite was such a vain woman I was sure this would woo her heart.

That evening, after she got home (late, naturally, she never would respect her curfew) I presented it to her.

For a moment her proud eyes softened.

"Oh Hephaestus," she gasped, "it's just beautiful!"

Then she kissed me.

Oh WOW!

I was so happy as I curled up on the cold floor that night. I was certain everything would be all right and that I and my princess would live happily ever after.

But maybe I *am* just a lame dingo with the mind of a wombat. That was the last time Aphrodite EVER kissed me.

Once she had that girdle she was more irresistible than ever. And instead of being grateful to me, she just used her upgraded power to get a whole lot more boyfriends.

You know, people say that my wife is the goddess of love. All I know is she was never very loving to me.

I rather think love might have less to do with physical beauty than we imagine. Maybe love is more about having a beautiful, kind heart.

Maybe love is more about respecting other people than using them.

If only we could find love like that on Mount Olympus.

Crikey mate, now that would be just bonza.

hapter four

The Hideous Horrid Headache
and the Bizarre Birth of Athena

One morning Zeus woke up with a terrible headache.

"Ooh!" he wailed. "I feel horrible! I feel as though someone is kicking the inside of my head with spikey shoes!"

"Ha!" snorted Hera unsympathetically. "Serves you right for getting sozzled with Dionysus last night!" She picked up a couple of frying pans and started whacking them together. "I hope this makes it much worse!" she yelled.

"STOP THAT, WOMAN!" screamed Zeus, holding his head tenderly. "It's not a hangover you idiot, it's MUCH worse!"

"So what!?" snorted Hera. "It can't be a worse headache than having to live with you forever!"

And she stomped off to do a spot of shopping. "He'll get over it!" she muttered as she bustled out of the door. "I'd never be so fortunate as to have him die. Immortality in a rotten husband is a real curse!"

But when she got back, Zeus hadn't gotten over it. He was lying on the floor and this is what he was saying.

"WAH WAH WAH WAH WAH WAH WAH WAH WAH!"

"Oh pull yourself together Zeus!" said Hera sternly. "You're a god aren't you? Show a little fortitude!"

"Ooh," sobbed Zeus. "Ooh, Hera it hurts quite horribly! Get me some help! Call an ambulance!"

"I don't know what an 'ambulance' is," grumbled Hera crossly, "but I'm going to get you some help so you can stop that stupid blubbering. It's frightfully undignified."

So she went out and rallied all the deities. They crowded into the palace and gawked at the pathetic sight of the mighty ruler of Heaven and Earth moaning and jerking with pain.

"Ha ha!" tittered Dionysus. "You did get a skin-full didn't you!"

"IT'S NOT A HANGOVER!" howled Zeus, "and I wish all of you would shut up your yapping and DO SOMETHING TO HELP ME!"

The ghastlies shrugged their shoulders helplessly. Although they were all adept in the graceful arts of fabrication, fornication and flatulence, not one of them knew how to heal a headache.

"Aaah!" shrieked Zeus in a tantrum of self-pity. "I'm your God! Why aren't you helping me! Why are you letting your all powerful and mighty ruler suffer like this!? Ooh, make it go away! **WAH WAH WAH WAH WAH WAH WAH!**"

"Oh don't start that again!" snarled Hera. "It goes through and through my head!"

"WHAT ABOUT MY HEAD!?" screamed Zeus, kicking his wife in the shins. "Ooh I think I'm going to die!"

"Oh, it's always just lovely promises and no action with you, isn't it Zeus!" shouted Hera, kicking her husband in the ribs.

The palace door swung open. Into the hall hobbled Hephaestus. He looked quite peeved. "Did you leave me off the party invite list *again* Mum?" he demanded crossly.

"This isn't a party," said Hera sternly, "and we've already explained to you why you aren't allowed at any parties. You're just too ugly."

Hephaestus scowled. Then he looked at Zeus lying in a puddle of his own dribble.

"What's wrong with Dad?" he asked.

"Oh don't worry about *him*," said Hera scornfully, "he's addled."

"Dear son," sniffed Zeus sadly, and he shot a nasty look at his wife, "death must visit even us immortals. The one thing you must never, ever forget, is that your father was always the greatest God that ever lived and your mother was a cantankerous shrew."

"WHAT?!" roared Hera. She flung herself on Zeus and began to smack his head.

"Aaaaaaaaaaaaaaaaaaaaaaaaaaaaaaaaaaaaaaaaaaaaa aaaaaaaaaaaaaaaaaaaaaaaaaaaaaaaaaaaaaaaaaah!" screamed Zeus. "Get this monster off me!"

Hephaestus looked at his mother. "Has he been out with Dionysus again?" he asked.

"I AM NOT DRUNK! I HAVE A HEADACHE!" roared Zeus in frustration.

"Oh well, I can fix that Dad!" said Hephaestus cheerfully.

"Really?!" yelped Zeus excitedly. "Oh my boy, HOW?"

"You have an ache in your head, so all we have to do is slice your head open and let the ache escape."

"Brilliant, brilliant, I love . . . . hang on a minute? Did you say 'slice' my head open?"

"Nothing to worry about Dad. It's a fairly simple medical procedure, it just involves an axe and a bit of force."

Zeus sat up. "I don't know about this, It doesn't sit quite right with me, I'll need to weigh up the pros and cons, check my insurance policy, ha ha, pardon me . . . ."

He started to crawl from the room, but Hera slammed her foot down on the edge of his tunic. "It's a glorious idea!" she announced. "Hephaestus, go and get your biggest axe, please."

"But Hera, my love," said Zeus nervously, "what if it goes wrong?"

"It can't go wrong. Either he does it right and you lose your biggest headache ever, or he does it wrong and I lose MY biggest headache ever. Either way, it's going to put a stop to your blubbing."

Hephaestus returned promptly looking very important. he carried a nice, newly sharpened axe.

"Right-o, Daddy!" he said encouragingly. "Just hold still. You may experience some cracking and ripping but it'll be over fairly fast."

"Son! No!" sobbed Zeus.

"Shut up Zeus!" said Hera callously. "It's for your own good."

Hephaestus rushed at his father, swinging the axe.

WAAAAAAAASH!

The axe smashed through Zeus's head and split it in half.

"Ha ha ha ha ha ha ha ha ha ha ha!" hooted Hera. "What a treat!" Then, hopefully, "Is he dead?"

"I am not dead!" said Zeus coldly. A dribble of blood was running down his face. "I don't actually think immortals can die after all. And I think that Hephaestus is a jolly rotten doctor."

Then something very strange began to happen. Zeus's head began to crack even further open.

"OW!" said Zeus.

"OUCH!" yelled Zeus.

"WAH WAH WAH WAH!" blubbered Zeus.

POP!

Out from Zeus's head leapt a fierce looking young woman. She was wearing a suit of armour and brandishing a spear.

"Greetings, Plebeians!" she boomed. "I come in potential peace. However, if you do not recognize me as the great warrior I am, I shall be obliged to slit you all from navel to nose!"

The ghastlies shuddered and nervously retreated.

Zeus, as he tried ineffectively to close his head, sat up and gaped at the cause of his headache.

"WELL!" said Zeus. "This explains everything! I was in labour! No wonder I felt so awful."

He looked reproachfully at his wife. "I do think you might have called for a midwife instead of bashing pots together and calling me unkind names!"

"Well, how was I to know you were pregnant?" scowled Hera, looking jealous. "I always thought men couldn't have babies."

"Not normally," agreed Zeus, "but apparently I'm a rather gifted man."

The ghastlies were getting acquainted with Zeus's daughter.

"My name is Athena," she told them. "I am the goddess of war."

"Oh wow, a career woman," mumbled the ghastlies, suitably impressed.

"So you're the goddess of war, eh?" snarled a nasty voice from the back of the hall. "And do you know who *I* am, mate?!"

"No," said Athena haughtily, "and I very much doubt I shall care."

"Oh I reckon you'll care, mate!" shouted the voice. "You're going to care, because I'M ARES, AND I'M ALREADY THE GOD OF WAR MATE!"

"Really?" sniffed Athena. "How quaint."

Ares stormed to the front of the hall. "You take that back or by crikey mate, I'm going to smash in your snotty little nose."

"Tsk, tsk," said Athena. "Just as I suspected, all brawn and no brains. I suppose you think battle is all about the killing and yahooing and seeing who managed to chop the most heads off!"

"I reckon it is mate!" yelled Ares, leaping up and down in excitement. "That's just bonza, mate!"

"*Don't* call me 'mate'." said Athena sternly. "I am not your 'mate'. I am not even your 'pal'. I am your rival, and it is my job to teach you that women can do anything men do, only we do it much better."

"OH YEAH!?" yelled Ares. "Come on then! Let's see who can break the most bones in a kickboxing contest!"

"No," said Athena contemptuously, "I prefer contests of a more academically rigorous nature."

"Chicken."

"I am no *Gallus domesticus,*" sniffed Athena scornfully. "I do not lay eggs, nor do I run away from noisy tyrants whose mouths are more full of words than their hearts are full of courage. I shall meet you as an equal on the field of battle. I shall surpass your greatest achievements and meet with fortitude the inevitable disenchantment that you will project upon me as a result of my supremacy in the arena of military strategy."

"Huh?" said Ares, looking confused.

Athena pushed her face into his. "I'm going to kick your rump!" she hissed.

Most brothers and sisters scrap a little bit but these two took it to an entirely new level.

And their father didn't help the situation at all. In fact, he made it much worse. Zeus was so chuffed that he'd given birth to a daughter he made quite a pet of her and favoured her with a special gift.

"WHAT?" screamed Ares. "Dad said you could use his thunderbolts?! That's blimmin unfair mate!"

"I suppose Dad loves me more," said Athena with a hateful little smile. "I suppose it's because I'm so beautiful and intelligent!"

"WHAT ABOUT ME?!" howled Ares. "I'M NICE LOOKING TOO!"

"Oh please," scoffed Athena. "You're a boy!"

"SO?!" yelled Ares, looking hurt. "WHAT'S THAT SUPPOSED TO MEAN?!"

"Ha ha" smirked Athena unkindly. "Ha ha ha!"

That was the last straw. Ares was so infuriated, he rushed off and started a war just to show his sister who was boss. And naturally, Athena rushed off to the war to show Ares that he WASN'T the boss.

Athena thought out her campaigns and reasoned why they were utterly necessary. She produced polished rhetoric about how ultimately everyone, including the victims of the war, would be so grateful for all the bloodshed. But she never took the time to ask the victims how grateful they actually were.

Ares didn't bother with all this thinking. "Pooh pooh!" he scoffed. "Who cares about the people! Let's get this war on the road! Let's get busy with the slaughter!"

"My war is good!" shouted Athena. "I uphold civilized standards! I'm a courteous General! You're just a butcher, Ares!"

"Whatever!" yelled Ares. "You're just a namby-pamby sook with nothing to fight for!"

"Unfeeling monster!"

"'Fraidie cat!"

"Humph!" snorted Athena as she flounced off to study military strategy. "My army is jolly lucky to have a intelligent, skilful leader like me!'

"Ha!" scoffed Ares as he stomped off to polish up his spear. "My army is blimmin fortunate to have a courageous, intrepid general like me!"

"My cause is just!" they both assured themselves smugly, "my war is a good war because my ideology is right!"

To generals there are always two kinds of war. Bad war and their war.

But to the people who have their farms turned into graveyards, their schools converted into prisons and their children killed, there is only ever the bad kind of war.

In the end, Athena proved to be the more competent leader and Ares sulkily returned to his recreational marauding. Athena smugly assumed her place as one of the most worshiped of the ghastlies.

No one seems to know what happened to Zeus and the problem of his severed head.

But he probably turned out just fine. After all, a caesarean may be a nasty business but considering that most women survive them, I dare say Zeus survived his.

After all, as he said himself, it does take a rather gifted man to give birth to his own daughter . . . .

Chapter Five

Pygmalion and the Stone Cold Maiden

Once upon a time there was a goldsmith called Pygmalion. His hobby was sculpting.

He lived in a house that overlooked the village. When he wasn't sculpting or gold-smithing he liked to look out his window and feel superior to the lowly occupants of the town.

He felt superior because they were all married and he was single.

Pygmalion didn't think much of marriage. Marriage meant having to share your house with a woman.

Love is in the Air!

Pygmalion did not like women. They talked too much, they were very opinionated and the ones in his village were very unfaithful.

Whatever you worship is what you will become. The woman of Pygmalion's village worshiped the awful, unfaithful, wanton goddess Aphrodite.

So naturally, they were all awful, unfaithful, wanton women.

Pygmalion was disgusted by them.

He looked down from his house and spat scornfully. "Yuck!" said Pygmalion, "I'm jolly glad I'm single."

He slammed the window shut and shot the bolt home.

"Good evening Pygmalion," said a sultry voice.

Pygmalion leapt into the air. "Yaaaaaaaah! Oh yuck! There's a *woman* in my house. I shall have to call the pest control."

"Pardon ME!" said the voice, and it sounded more angry than sultry this time, "I am no mere woman. I am the beautiful, the gorgeous, the stunning, the simply dazzling Miss Aphrodite."

"Oh GROSS!" Pygmalion shouted. "You're the worst of them all!"

"Silence, oh ungrateful man!" snarled Aphrodite, striding towards him. "Why haven't you got married?"

She pushed her divinely lovely countenance into Pygmalion's horrified face. "Tell me Pygie," she cooed with a flutter of her eyelashes, "is it because you want one just like me?"

"Oh heck," growled Pygmalion, "I'm trying to *avoid* getting one like YOU."

"*What?*" roared Aphrodite.

"You're a jolly nasty piece of work. I know how you treat your own husband."

"THOU SHALL MARRY, OH HORRID LITTLE MAN!" screamed Aphrodite in a towering rage. "HOW DARE THOU JUDGE ME, THOU POLTROON?!"

Now when a goddess starts talking like a Shakespearian sonnet, you know you have a problem. And given that the average magic arsenal of a goddess is generally larger than that of a goldsmith, Pygmalion thought it would behove him to tread with caution.

"Well, Aphrodite," he said carefully, "when you put it like that, I can see your point. And I certainly appreciate you coming all the way from Mount Olympus to tell me. But having actually seen you creates quite a problem."

"Oh?"

"Well, you are reasonably pretty . . ."

"Ahem?"

"Very pretty. Well anyway, how will I ever be happy with a mortal after seeing you?"

"That is a very good point and I feel compassion for your predicament. I suppose compared with me, any other woman would be hideously ugly."

"Don't count on it."

"Pardon?"

"Oh absolutely, you summed it up beautifully."

"Dear mortal, what can I do for you, to mitigate the agony you must feel at not being able to obtain me?"

"Oh gosh Aphrodite, I don't know. I guess you could give me time to recover."

"And how long would that take, dear one?"

"Not long."

"Pardon?"

"Oh, ages, eons. Err, if you gave me time to carve a statue of you, it might help."

"Ah I understand. So when you are married, you can still look at me."

"Yuck."

"What?"

"Yes, yes you've summed it up perfectly."

So Aphrodite left for Mount Olympus and Pygmalion opened all the windows in his house to get rid of the awful stench of her perfume. Then he lugged out a really enormous block of marble.

Pygmalion had no intention of ever marrying. He knew that Aphrodite was a twit when it came to her looks and he knew that she would never interfere with a statue being made of her. And Pygmalion had a cunning plan. He wasn't going to EVER finish his statue. He could stretch it out for infinity.

This worked just fine for a while. But as is the custom with most artists, Pygmalion got very caught up in his project. He wanted it finished so he could admire what he had made. Quite probably he also wanted the lump of marble out of his living room. Such an inconvenience.

Also, the statue was looking less and less like Aphrodite. And that was, Pygmalion felt, a vast improvement.

It didn't have her nasty piggy, proud eyes.

It didn't have her horrid big bright red lips.

Best of all, it didn't have her obnoxious bossy voice.

Yes, Pygmalion had done it. He had created the perfect woman.

His darling was beautiful, faithful (she never even left the house!) and best of all, oh the crème de la crème! His darling was utterly, totally SILENT!

Wow, you talk about a blessing!

Unfortunately, all this success went straight to Pygmalion's brain and it addled his mind.

He started to court his big marble doll with a ridiculous amount of passion. He brought her flowers and she gazed impassively at them with her lovely marble eyes.

He brought her fruit but her beautiful mouth couldn't taste anything.

He told her he loved her and she ignored him.

Most men would have been put off by this chilly reception, but it only increased Pygmalion's devotion.

He started to talk to her. She was a jolly good listener.

"Can I kiss you darling?" he asked his statue hopefully, after he had presented her with a golden necklace.

His darling didn't say anything.

"If you *don't* want me to kiss you," said Pygmalion cunningly, "just say so."

His darling didn't answer.

"Ah ha!" ogled Pygmalion. "Ah ha, I knew it, I knew it! My sweetheart is such a coy little thing!"

Then he gave her a big smooch on her frozen lips.

It wasn't nearly as enjoyable as he had thought it was going to be. It was just like kissing a marble rolling pin.

"Why so cold my dove?" gasped Pygmalion. "Are you ill, my pet? Perhaps you need to go to bed."

Pygmalion grabbed his statue and began to drag it towards the bedroom. She was very, very heavy.

"My dear," panted Pygmalion, "for one so delicate, you weigh a ton."

He hoofed her onto the bed. The bed promptly broke.

"Oh darling!" wailed a distraught Pygmalion. "Did that hurt, my precious?!"

His statue gazed impassively at him.

"Sweetheart," soothed Pygmalion, "your dear own Pygie will make it all better."

He began to pile quilts on his statue, but she remained as cold as a marble stone. Because, actually, that was what she was.

"My love!" sobbed Pygmalion. "You have a fever, I am sure you will die. Wait, maybe if I cuddle you, you will feel warmer."

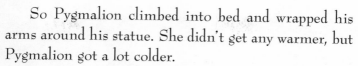

So Pygmalion climbed into bed and wrapped his arms around his statue. She didn't get any warmer, but Pygmalion got a lot colder.

"D-d-d-d-d-darling," he shivered "I'm so c-c-c-c-c-cold, your skin is so i-i-i-cy."

Poor old Pygmalion. It's jolly hard work to keep loving someone who doesn't love you back.

In the morning Pygmalion was frozen cold. He was also desperate.

Being so chilly had knocked a bit of sense into his head and he had realized that his wife was nothing more than a pretty piece of white marble.

So despite loathing Aphrodite and all the woman under her jurisdiction, he bought a bunch of roses and set off to pray a prayer at Aphrodite's festival.

Aphrodite was in a very good mood. People had been telling her all day how beautiful she was, and although she already knew it, she did so love a good big dose of flattery now and then.

When she saw Pygmalion coming she was even more pleased.

"Hello Hoggy." She said.

"Huh?" said Pygmalion.

"Pygmalion, Pygie, pig, hog hoggy, ha ha, get it?" sniggered Aphrodite.

"Not really," said Pygmalion.

"Oh well, you humans are just so much dumber than us gods."

"I suppose you're here to worship me Pygie?"

"Yeah, sort of," mumbled Pygmalion.

Aphrodite stood up and waved her arms graciously. "Proceed to admire my great worth and beauty, oh worthless and not beautiful human."

"Um, thanks," said Pygmalion unenthusiastically. "Um, I brought you some roses."

"Oh, for me?" gasped Aphrodite. "Oh Pygmalion, you should have."

"I know," grunted Pygmalion.

"Ahh," said Aphrodite. "You are sad."

"Yeah, how did you know?"

"My dear chap, I am a goddess. I can always tell when people are sad and I always know why they are sad."

Pygmalion was strangely touched. Aphrodite sounded almost kind.

He sniffed sadly. "I'm very sad Aphrodite, very, very sad."

"Yes, you are sad because you see that you and I can never be together."

"*What!?*"

Aphrodite held out her palm. "Hush, dear heart. It could never work. It's nothing personal, it's just that you are so hideously ugly I couldn't stand to have you as my boyfriend."

Pygmalion's mouth fell open in shock.

"Silence thy grieving heart," continued Aphrodite, "for although I cannot give you the thing you long for, I will give you a small consolation. Go home, for the statue of me has become a woman for you to love."

A wave of euphoria washed over Pygmalion. Tears of joy began to course down his cheeks.

Aphrodite began to sob too. "Go, dear heart!" she cried. "At least you can *pretend* you are married to me. Go quickly, run, run I tell you, for compassion for your distress is blinding my eyes to your yucky looks. And if you were to beseech me once more for my love I feel sure it would be yours!"

That woke Pygmalion up! He leapt into the air and *raced* home as fast as his ugly legs could carry him.

Aphrodite watched him go with affection. "Such a noble soul," she sniffed, "denying his heart to spare me from having to suffer an ugly boyfriend!"

Pygmalion ran into his house. There sat his wife. Warm, rosy and soft. He had got his wish.

Pygmalion and Galatea (that was her name) seemed to have lived happily ever after. Quite an accomplishment in a world where most married couples spent their lives cheating, murdering and child eating.

So maybe all that waiting paid off in the end.

Pygmalion loved his wife. In fact there was just one little, tiny problem. Galatea might have been whole lot more fun to kiss nowadays, but alas, that monument of perfection, her silence, was never to be recovered.

"Oh well, never mind," thought Pygmalion, "she's beautiful, honest and true. That's all the perfection I need."

And he went off into his workshop and carved himself a nice pair of earmuffs.

Chapter Six

A Very Creepy Love Story

Horrible old Hades was the king of the Underworld. He was a dark surly fellow, but let's not judge him too harshly for his sulky disposition.

He was part of the famous Titan Dynasty, a sort of old-boys network made up of some of the most famous gods.

When the regions of the earth were carved up, his brother Poseidon got the sparkling oceans and his other brother Zeus got the sky and the thrill of being the CEO of Mount Olympus.

"Well, what do I get then?" asked Hades hopefully.

"Ha ha," smirked Poseidon.

"Ho ho," sniggered Zeus.

"Come on you guys," grinned Hades excitedly, "you can tell me!"

"Oh we have a special assignment for you Hades, don't we Poseidon?"

"Ha ha you bet!"

"Well?!" gasped Hades, bouncing up and down with enthusiasm.

"It's just perfect for you," said Zeus with a mean little smile, "we've decided to make you a King."

"Oh, me, really? A King!?"

"You are going to the King of the Underworld!"

"WHAT?!" screamed Hades.

"Oh just think of the benefits of being King of the Dead, Hades!" said Poseidon in an encouraging voice. "You'll have no revolutions or rebellions to put down! You won't have the bother of having execute any of your subjects because they'll already be dead!"

"Then YOU be King of the Underworld!" screamed Hades in fury. "I don't want to!"

"Too bad for you then," said Zeus coldly, "because that's all you're gonna get mate."

So while Zeus went off to an executive board meeting and Poseidon went off to court a beautiful sea nymph, poor old Hades climbed down a grave to investigate his new job.

It wasn't encouraging. It mainly involved overseeing the placement of coffins and granting haunting rights to a few lucky spirits who still wanted go tramping about the world.

"Oh great," said Hades sarcastically "just what I always wanted, a bunch of dead people to talk to."

He emerged from his chilly domain. He looked jealously at the Overworld.

"Well this stinks," he growled. "I thought being a god was supposed to be fun."

He was in the middle of a paddock filled with wildflowers. "Ha!" growled Hades, "it's so unfair! All the other gods are surrounded by beauty. Me? I'm surrounded by caskets and ghosts. What a life."

Then he noticed something even prettier than the flowers. Climbing a style into the paddock was a young woman. She was lovely to look at and Hades suddenly had an idea.

"If I have to live with a bunch of dead people," he growled to himself, "I'm jolly well not going to it alone."

And he stormed off to find Zeus.

"Zeus!" he yelled, exploding into the executive board meeting. "Get over here, I want to talk to you!"

"Not now Hades!" snarled Zeus, "can't you see I'm in the middle of something?"

"Zeus!" shrieked Hades. "Get over here before I knock your block off! You blimmin well owe me five minutes after the stinking trick you played me!"

"Pardon me gentlemen," said Zeus, "I must attend to my idiot brother. He's clearly deranged and he won't leave until I humour him."

"What do you want, you twit?" hissed Zeus angrily. "And why aren't you cataloguing dead people?"

"I want a wife!" yelled Hades. "I want a pretty wife so I have something to love. You owe me that much!"

"Oh pooh!" said Zeus, "you don't need a wife, there must be thousands of women in your Kingdom!"

"Yeah!" screamed Hades, "thousands of DEAD ones!"

"Oh wah wah wah wah," said Zeus. "That's what I hate about you Hades, the glass is always half empty with you isn't it?"

"Listen Zeus," shouted Hades in fury, "you're married to a goddess, you date supermodels and you get to run Mount Olympus. All I want is one reasonably pretty girl that isn't decomposing."

"Oh all right then you little twerp," shrugged Zeus. "Who do you want?"

"That dainty little thing that keeps visiting the wildflower meadow."

"Persephone? Demeter's daughter? Well, for a twerp you certainly have good taste. All right Hades, you can marry her. Now be a good chap and go away, you're lowering the real-estate value."

Hades was very pleased with the outcome of his conversation with Zeus. That would show Zeus that just because he was the head god didn't mean he got to call all the shots.

Hades waited for Persephone the next day. When she came dancing into the field, he charged out of the underworld in a great, horrible hearse pulled by six enormous black stallions.

He grabbed her and flung her into the hearse. Naturally, Persephone started to scream and shriek in terror.

Hades whacked his stallions into a gallop and they all charged down into the Underworld. The door slammed shut behind them.

Hades halted his stallions and leapt down to help Persephone out of the hearse. This did not go well.

"Aaaaah!" screamed Persephone in horror. "Oh help! I've been kidnapped by a horrible demon!"

Hades, in a romantic fervour, tried to slide his arm around her waist. Persephone began to kick him.

Hades didn't particularly like to restrain his bride, but he was in danger of losing all his teeth so he grabbed her arms and pinned them to her sides.

"I'm not a horrible demon," he reassured her. "I'm the King of the Underworld."

"Aaaaaaaaaaaaaaaaaaaaaaaaaaaaaaaaaaaaaaaaaa aaaaaaaaaaaaaaaaaaaaaaaaaaaaaaaaaaaaah!" screamed Persephone. "I've been kidnapped by the grim reaper!"

"No darling, no you haven't been," panted Hades as he managed to get a head lock on her, "I'm not going to hurt you my love, just marry you."

"Aaaaaaaaaaaaaaaaaaaaaaaaaaaaaaaaaaaaaaaaaa aaaaaaaaaaaaaaaaaaaaaaaaaaaaaaaaaaaaah!" screamed Persephone, biting his shoulder. "Boo hoo, I've been abducted by a ghost!"

Hades sighed. Nothing seemed to be going well for him. Restraining her as gently as he could, he carried her into his living room. He set her down on the sofa.

"Calm down darling," he said, "I'll get you a nice cup of tea."

"I don't want a cup of tea," sobbed Persephone. "I want my Mum!"

"Now dear," said Hades, reminding himself that he was the man, and thus must take charge, "it's going to be all right love, there's nothing to be afraid of."

"I'M IN HELL!" screamed Persephone in fury. "THERE'S EVERYTHING TO BE AFRAID OF!"

"Shh," soothed Hades, "it's not as bad as all that, my dear." He set a mug of tea in front of her.

"YOU ARE USING A COFFIN AS A TEA TABLE!" bawled Persephone, stamping her feet in rage.

And so it went on, day after day after day.

Hades was as kind as kind could be to Persephone, but women are complex beings and there is something about being dragged down into a grave that tends to squelch their romantic side.

"Darling," said Hades with tender concern, "you haven't touched your dinner."

"I shall never eat anything prepared in this squalor!" retorted Persephone with vim.

She had realized that Hades really wasn't going to hurt her, and so she had stopped being afraid and started to be very cantankerous.

"How would you like a kiss?" asked Hades, gazing wistfully at Persephone's beautiful face.

"How would you like a smack in the mouth!?" snapped Persephone.

Upstairs in the Overworld, things weren't going so well either. Demeter was distraught about the loss of her precious daughter.

"Boo hoo!" she sobbed. "Where can my darling daughter have wandered off to?"

She hunted high and low but to no avail. After ten days a rather reclusive goddess, Hecate, who lived in a dingy subdivision of the Underworld arrived at Demeter's door.

"I've got some news for you about Persephone," she mumbled.

"Oh Zeus be praised!" sobbed Demeter.

"Oh, I wouldn't go that far," warned Hecate. "As a matter of fact, it's sort of his fault she disappeared in the first place."

When Demeter found out that Zeus had given her daughter to the Lord of the Dead, she was furious. And a furious mother is one nature's nastiest weapons.

"OH HE DID, DID HE?" she roared. "WELL, WE'LL JOLLY WELL SEE ABOUT THAT!"

Back in the underworld Hades was getting more and more glum. Persephone was showing no sign of weakening in her determination to never love him, and as for the subject of marriage . . . .

"I shall NEVER, NEVER, NEVER, NEVER marry you!" swore Persephone vehemently. "Never, not even if you were the last man in the cosmos!"

Up at Mount Olympus, Zeus was at yet another executive board meeting. He simply loved attending them. If anyone brought up a suggestion he didn't like, he just zapped them with his thunderbolts. Oh it was jolly good fun!

"Gentlemen," he was saying, "I propose that we change the name of Mount Olympus to 'Zeus Mountain'. I feel that this would greatly increase our marketability and . . . ."

"ZEUS!" screamed Demeter, bursting into the room. "Get over here, I need to talk to you!"

"Not now Demeter!" snapped the CEO of Mount Olympus. "Can't you see I'm in the middle of something?"

"OH you're in the middle of something alright!" snarled Demeter, "and if you don't get yourself over here pronto, you're liable in be in the middle of a full body cast too!"

"Excuse me gentlemen," growled Zeus, "yet another lunatic for me to humour . . . ."

"Well, what do you want?" He hissed at Demeter as he hustled her out of the room.

"YOU GAVE MY BABY GIRL TO HADES!" shouted Demeter. "You gave my daughter to the Lord of the Dead!"

"So what?!" snapped Zeus. "You interrupted my executive board meeting for *that*?"

"Oh you're going to pay, Zeus. You think you can do whatever you want, and because you run this place it's ok. But you have crossed the line this time mate, and you are going to deeply regret messing with my daughter."

"Ah ha ha," said Zeus nervously. "Um, what do you mean by that, Demeter?"

"I'm the goddess of agriculture, and as long as my darling daughter stays under the ground, then so shall all the crops. Not one farmer is going to harvest so much as a melon, as long as Persephone remains with Hades."

"Oh big whoop!" snorted Zeus, "so you're gonna inconvenience a few farmers? Who cares, I loathe farming anyway, it's such a worthless, dirty pursuit."

"Oh you think so, do you?" Demeter asked quietly.

"Oh sure, farming is for losers who aren't smart enough to become big, important CEOs like me!"

"Very well Zeus," said Demeter softly. "We shall see how well a big, important CEO copes when the farmers fail."

And she walked steadily from the room.

"What a loser!" yelled Zeus, and he went back to his big, important, executive board meeting.

Beware of a person's rage. But be warier still of their self control.

Demeter went home, folded her arms and waited. When the spring arrived and people planted their seeds, she did not whisper to the seeds in the moonlight, encouraging them to grow.

When the summer came she did not call on the rain to nurture the tender shoots.

When the autumn came she sang no songs of growth to the vines.

And when the winter came, the people starved.

The famine affected even the gods. And Persephone, who had refused to eat when there was plenty was afflicted with terrible hunger now that there was nothing.

"Persephone?" whispered Hades softly. "I found the last pomegranate in the world, I thought you might like it."

Persephone was touched. Hades wasn't looking so healthy himself but he had brought the last pomegranate to her.

She took a bite. Then she gasped. "Hades!" she gulped, "doesn't a pomegranate mean marriage?"

Hades shrugged. "I suppose so, but it hardly matters, it looks as though we're all going to die anyway."

He kissed her gently, and for once, Persephone did not shove him away.

Meanwhile, in the Overworld, something very strange was happening.

The big, important CEO of Mount Olympus was sitting in Demeter's tiny cottage bawling his eyes out.

"WAAAAAAAAAAAAAAAH!" he blubbered. "There's no more food!"

"How interesting," remarked Demeter.

"I'm SO hungry!" howled Zeus.

"Really?" asked Demeter.

"And I'm so stressed!" he bawled, blowing his big, important, executive nose loudly.

This seemed to genuinely interest Demeter. "And why is that, Zeus?"

"Oh I have all these beastly prayers to deal with! It's all 'I'm hungry Zeus, I can't feed my family Zeus, do something Zeus!' Don't these people realize I've got my own problems?!"

"I thought you were a big, important CEO Zeus," said Demeter sternly. "I thought farming was for losers who couldn't aspire to your elevated position in society."

"I was wrong!" sobbed Zeus. "Farmers are the backbone of society! There, I said it, are you happy now?!"

"Not quite! I didn't start this famine because of your beastly, ignorant, arrogant view of yourself, and even though I'm very happy that you are now a much wiser, humbled CEO, I STILL WANT MY DAUGHTER BACK!"

"Anything, anything!" moaned Zeus, "just as long as I don't have to listen to any more whinging and complaining about starving to death. People can be *so* inconsiderate!"

"Tell me about it," snorted Demeter, glaring at him.

Zeus summoned Hades and Persephone to the Overworld.

"My daughter!" sobbed Demeter flinging her arms around Persephone. "My darling child!"

"Hello Mum," said Persephone weakly.

Demeter scowled at Hades. "I'd like to ship you off as an inmate to the Underworld, you fiend."

"The deal's off Hades," said Zeus, "you have to give her back."

Hades shuffled his feet and looked sad. Persephone looked at him, and then she looked at her mother.

"Mum," she said nervously. "I got so hungry I ate a pomegranate down there. And that means I'm his wife now doesn't it?"

"Not in this instance!" said Demeter, stroking Persephone's hair and beaming a deathly glance at Hades. "We'll just ignore the law this time sweetheart."

A big tear rolled down Hades' face. He started to creep out of the room.

"Mum," said Persephone even more nervously, "Mum, he's not a bad sort really."

Hades stopped in his tracks.

"Mum, I don't think I want to leave him anymore."

Hades gasped. Then he started to smile. And when he smiled, he didn't look nearly as creepy as he usually did.

"Darling, NO!" cried Demeter. "We can't allow you back into his evil clutches!"

"Mum, he had me down there for a whole year and he never did anything nasty. He can't help it that his brothers were selfish and made him take the worst job."

Zeus started to go a bit red.

"Hmm," said Demeter. "Well, he certainly does have a horrid brother."

Zeus scowled.

"Darling," said Demeter, "I'm glad you weren't mistreated, but even if Hades does love you and you love him, you simply can't go back because when you are away from me I can't find the heart to make anything grow."

"Oh boring!" yelled Zeus. "Again with *farming*, how yucky, how . . . ." He caught Demeter's eye and trailed off.

"Well Zeus," said Hades, "what should we do? I mean, you are the CEO of Mount Olympus, after all."

"True," said Demeter. "Not a very good one, not nearly as important as you think you are, and certainly no farmer, but you are the CEO. What do you think we should do?"

"Oh I say," said Zeus in delight at being asked, "I say . . . ."

"*Well*?" snapped Demeter. "What *do* you say?"

"Oh! I say, I say, that you ought to share Persephone between you. You can have half a year each." He grinned sheepishly. "Does that work?"

"Not too bad for a mere executive," said Demeter politely.

And that is what happened. Demeter had Persephone for one half of the year and Hades had her for the other half.

You can tell when Persephone is out and about with her mother. The earth laughs with flowers and fruit.

And when it gets chilly and bleak, then you know she's keeping Hades company underground.

And what happened to the CEO of Mount Olympus?

Well, it's awfully hard to humble a god, and Zeus rather quickly forgot about his tiff with Demeter.

But any time he starts to swank about how he has a big, important job, Demeter just smiles and says, "Oh well, we can't all be farmers can we?"

And Zeus slinks off to his board meeting feeling very, very silly.

# hapter Seven

Evil Eos and her
Crackpot Courtship

Back in the day when the ghastly gods ruled the world there was a grubby little goddess called Eos.

Eos doesn't get quite as much attention as some of the big ghastlies but she was every bit as nasty.

She was totally boy crazy and instead of using her divine power to influence the world for good Eos just wasted all her time collecting boyfriends.

One day as she looked down from her lofty, godly home, she spied a terrifically handsome human.

"Wow!" boomed ghastly little Eos. "What a looker! I simply must have him for my man collection!"

Poor old Tithonus, he came from a tribe of good lookers, and the gods were always pinching members of his family.

In fact Tithonus probably already had a girlfriend, given his good looks, but these silly little ethical problems never seemed to bother the ghastlies.

So Eos just swooped down like a great big hawk and snatched Tithonus up to her cloudy domain.

"Hello Handsome!" she yelled at him. "Bet you never thought you'd get kidnapped by a goddess eh?!"

"Oh no!" growled Tithonus. "The beastly god plague strikes again, I've been caught! Blast my incredibly attractive physique!"

"Hey!" snarled Eos. "Watch it mate, I'm no gorgon myself, in case you hadn't noticed, I'M A GODDESS!"

"Yeah," Tithonus grumbled, "but you ain't no Aphrodite either."

"Ooh you watch your mouth you ungrateful wallaby!" screamed Eos. "I'm about sick of Ares yapping on about that sleazy shark and I'm blimmin well not going to stand for it in my husband, matey!"

"Your husband?" gulped Tithonus nervously. "Um, don't you think you'd rather just pick a nice looking god and return me to earth?"

"*NO!*" snarled Eos. "Gods are so dreadfully bossy, but I shall be able to control YOU!"

"Uh oh."

"Yeah that's right mate, I'm a goddess and that means I'm jolly well going to wear the pants in this marriage!"

"What if I kick the bucket? Wouldn't you be happier with an immortal?"

"He he," giggled Eos. "I've worked out how to fix that. Come on mate, you and I are going to spend an eternity together."

And so saying she grabbed him in her burly grip and hauled him off to see Zeus.

"Hey Zeus!" roared Eos. "Look what I found! Can I keep him?!"

"Oh whatever," yawned Zeus. "You usually do, Eos."

"Yeah," agreed Eos, "but I want to keep this one for ever Zeus, and humans are generally so disposable. I want this one preserved."

"Immortality Eos? Don't tell me you're going in for all that 'faithful 'til death' stuff. What a bore."

"Listen," yelled Eos, "I don't want him to die, I want him to live forever so I can always have someone handy to boss around!"

"Ha, ha" Zeus laughed. "Megalomania, excessive control disorder, I love it! Very well Eos, you may keep your *Homo sapien*. He is now immortal. Enjoy yourself. Ha ha."

"Oh no," groaned poor Tithonus.

"Come on husband!" boomed Eos. "Time to go on honeymoon!"

"Ha ha ha!" sniggered Zeus. "Ha ha, jolly good show by Jove!"

So off on their honeymoon Eos dragged poor old Tithonus and from there into their everlasting, eternal marriage.

And for the first few years this went rather well for Eos. No one seems to have bothered to record how much Tithonus enjoyed his side of the marriage.

In any case I'm sure we can guess. How would YOU like to be forced into an eternal marriage with an unbearably bossy goddess?

But one day Eos noticed something odd. "Tithonus," she said in surprise "Are you gaining weight?"

"How should I know?" growled Tithonus sulkily.

"Yes, I believe you are! And whatever has happened to all your lovely hair Tithonus?"

"It's been falling out. I suppose it's the stress of living with you for eternity," grunted Tithonus unkindly.

"Ugh, and the few bits you have left are GREY Tithonus, by Zeus, they're GREY!!!!!!!!"

"Stress can do that too," muttered Tithonus crossly.

"And your face, oh Tithonus it's so ugly and lined! Oh Tithonus you're OLD! Oh gross, my husband is OLD! I'm married to a yucky old man!"

Eos ran to Zeus. "My husband is OLD!" She screamed. "Oh it's just disgusting! I'm married to a bald old man!"

"Ha ha jolly good show by Jove!" roared Zeus smacking his knee in glee. "Ha ha you didn't ask for eternal beauty did you? Just eternal life! He He! And if you don't like the middle age spread just you wait 'til he goes senile! Ha ha ha!"

"Senile?!" Screamed Eos. "Eww, I'm not going to put up with that, mate!"

"Ho ho I don't see how you'll avoid it!" hooted Zeus. "You'll never get rid of him!"

"Yeah right mate!" roared Eos. "I'm not going to have an ugly old husband dribbling all over my house for eternity!"

She went home. "The marriage is annulled!" she told Tithonus. "I need to be free to find a new, young, glamorous husband."

And she dragged poor old Tithonus over to her closet, flung him in, locked the door and threw the key away.

Tithonus went quite mad. He babbled away for years, and then he underwent a metamorphosis and became a cicada.

You might think this is a horrible ending for poor old Tithonus, but I rather think it was a lovely ending.

You see, it enabled him to choose a new wife. And as everybody knows, with cicadas, only the male cicada ever does the talking.

In fact, maybe the Romans, who came along a great deal later, were thinking of Tithonus when they remarked (rather rudely I'm afraid) "Happy is the cicada, for his woman is silent!"

hapter Eight

Drunken Dionysus And The Birth Of Booze

Drunken Dionysus had a rough start in life. Most alcoholics do.

His pa was the philandering Zeus. Philandering is a big word and people like to use it because it so nicely obscures what philandering really is.

Philandering means cheating on your spouse with lots and lots of different people.

Philandering isn't a very nice thing.

One day Zeus decided to go philandering with a beautiful princess called Semele.

Poor old Semele probably just thought she'd married a lovely steady chap who was utterly devoted to her. Unfortunately that 'lovely steady chap' was already married.

Even worse, his real wife was Hera. And Hera was just about fed up with Zeus and all his girlfriends.

She'd tried discussing his wanton ways in a discreet and civilized manner. It went like this. "Zeus! Where are you going tonight?!"

"NONE OF YOUR BUSINESS, WOMAN!"

"I believe you've got a new girlfriend! Oh Zeus, how can you be so unkind?!"

"SHUT YOUR FACE WOMAN!"

"Zeus, I've never once cheated on you! Why do you insist on cheating on me?"

"BECAUSE I WANT TO, YOU OLD BAT FACE! IT'S FUN!!!"

This could have gone on forever but Zeus didn't have time for all this tedious communicating with his wife, so he simply fixed the problem by bashing her in the jaw so she couldn't do any more whinging.

Charming husband huh?

And off he went to his human wife Semele.

Eventually Semele got pregnant. Zeus was rather pleased. Goodness knows why, he certainly doesn't sound like very good daddy material to ME.

Hera didn't relish the concept of another bash in the jaw and for all its finery Mount Olympus didn't have a women's refuge. So she decided to extract her revenge from poor old Semele.

She wandered down to earth and banged on Semele's door.

Semele opened the door. She had a belly the size of a watermelon.

Hera ground her teeth into a fake smile. "Hello dear," she said.

"Hi," grinned Semele. "Would you like to come in? I'll just pop the kettle on."

"Thank you dear," snarled Hera. She sat down on a chair. "Where's your husband dear?" she asked.

"Oh I don't know." smiled poor, foolish Semele as she poured tea for Hera. "He commutes a long way for work."

"I bet he does," growled Hera.

"He's so sweet," blushed Semele. "He's so devoted to me."

"How *nice*!"

Semele gazed at Hera with her big, innocent eyes. "What's your name? I'm Semele."

"Ha! I know that. I've come to tell you something just lovely dear."

"Oh really, how exciting."

"Oh it's exciting all right." muttered Hera through gritted teeth. "Your husband is not what he says he is, my dear."

"Oh?"

"Ha ha no. In fact you are going to get quite a zap when you find out what he really is. Yes, it'll be an electric moment."

"Oh dear this is all so exciting! What is my husband REALLY?!"

"A real creep."

"Pardon?"

"Oh I can't tell you that my dear. I'd simply loathe to ruin the surprise. Just ask him to show himself to you in his TRUE colours."

"He he," thought Hera. "That ought to do it!"

"Oh thank you, dear old lady!"

"Oh no my dear, *thank you!*"

That evening when Zeus arrived at the home of his earthly wife she gave him a big kiss. "Hello Bob dear, did you have a nice day at the office?"

"Oh very nice," said Bob dear, sitting down to a scrummy dinner and thinking how nice it was to have a human wife who didn't consider herself above cooking.

"Bob dear, you do love me don't you?" asked Semele coyly, as she twisted her beautiful hair about her dainty fingers.

"Sweetheart!" yelled Zeus through a mouthful of chicken pie, "you are the bee's knees, the cat's whiskers and I'll give you anything you want! Just name it Baby, and it's yours!"

"Oh darling, how nice!" cried Semele flinging her arms about his neck "because there is one thing . . . ."

"Shoot Love, it's yours."

Dumb, dumb, dumb Zeus. Some god, he couldn't see just five minutes into his own future.

"Darling, I want to see you in your true form."

"OH NO! NOT THAT!" yelled Zeus.

"But darling," crooned Semele nuzzling his neck "you promised."

"Uh, no, I didn't," lied Zeus.

"Oh, but darling you did. You said I was the cat's whiskers and the bee's knees and I could have anything I wanted."

And Semele began to cry.

"Oh Tristan, oh Isolde!" groaned Zeus, wringing his hands. "Sweetheart, you don't understand!"

"Oh yes I do Bob!" sniffed Semele crossly. "You're not a man of your word!"

Now this was quite true. Zeus wasn't a man of his word. He wasn't even a god of his word. But he was a very proud, arrogant god and Semele had pricked his pride.

"ALL RIGHT BABY!" he screamed, "YOU ASKED FOR IT AND YOU ARE GONNA GET IT!"

ZAAAAAAP!

Hera was right. It WAS an electric moment. Zeus, in a towering rage exploded into a bolt of lightning and consumed poor Semele in fire.

Pretty soon all that was left of the lovely Semele was a tiny pile of charcoal. For some reason the foetus had survived, and as I have said, Zeus was quite looking forward to being a daddy.

"Golly, at least I've got THAT!" said Zeus, and he snatched his son up.

"Hmm, this baby isn't full term, what shall I do?" he asked himself.

You know, it's a worrying thing when your god is a god of very little brain.

"Ooh I know!" beamed Zeus, "I'll carry him to term!"

Then his brow furrowed. "No, wait, pregnancy is more of a lady thing isn't it? Oh dear, what to do, what to do . . . ."

Then his noble, intellectual face cleared. "Ah ha!" he shouted exuberantly. "I shall be the first daddy ever, to be pregnant with his own son!"

He took out his pocket knife and chopped a big hole in his hip. Then he grabbed Dionysus and jammed him into the hole.

"Oh, I'm a genius!" chortled Zeus with supreme self-satisfaction as he sewed his son into his leg.

So without the benefits of a womb or an umbilical cord, little Dionysus grew on and on in his daddy's hip.

Eventually even Zeus got fed up with the novelty of being a pregnant daddy and proceeded to chop into the enormous canker on his leg.

Out popped Dionysus. "Hi Mum, what's up?" he asked Zeus.

"My boy!" boomed Zeus with pride. "I am not your Mum, I'm your Dad, son!"

"That's cool dude." Dionysus said. "So what's this junk heap called?"

"This," smirked Zeus, "is Zeus mountain! Some people call it Mount Olympus, but I think Zeus mountain has a more classy ring to it. Don't you agree?"

"I'm cool with that dude," said Dionysus, "whatever floats your boat."

"Well son," said Zeus, "now that you're born, where would you like to hang out with your (ha ha) old man?"

"Maybe later, Dude," said Dionysus, shrugging his shoulders. "Right now I feel like inventing a mind altering substance with the potential to wreak marriages and destroy families."

"Oh son!" sniffed Zeus dabbing at his eyes. "Daddy is so proud of his ambitious little boy."

But unfortunately Hera had overheard the whole conversation.

"I'll not have that illegitimate little toad around here," she snarled, quite forgetting that it wasn't Dionysus' fault that he was illegitimate. Jealousy can make one very unreasonable. It can also make one very evil.

Hera gathered the Titans, a warlike siblinghood of old, aristocratic gods. "Listen to me," she muttered, "that Dionysus has got to go! He's bad news, I tell you!"

"Ha ha!" laughed the Titans. "This situation calls for a spot of cannibalism!"

So they waited until Zeus had popped out to get yet another girlfriend, and they grabbed Dionysus.

"Yum yum!" giggled those terrible Titans. "Curried baby, just what we like!"

But as they simmered garlic and ginger in a skillet of olive oil and prepared to chop Dionysus up, another Titan who doesn't seem to have been quite so terrible came along.

"Why is that baby lying on the chopping board?" demanded Rhea sternly, "and why are you rubbing him with rosemary?"

And she took Dionysus away from them.

For a while Rhea dressed Dionysus as a girl and hid him in a king's palace, but Hera found out about it and Dionysus had to move on.

So off into the world went Dionysus. After a while he stumbled upon a grape vine. "Wow, this has potential!" said Dionysus. "If I just rot a few of these purple round things down and get it into a liquid form I reckon I'll have created my mind altering substance!"

Well, it turned out to be slightly more complicated than that, but Dionysus was certainly shooting in the right direction.

After a bit of experimentation Dionysus won the dubious honour of having invented alcohol.

He taught the art to a farmer called Icarius who was most appreciative, and who promptly threw a drunken party for all his friends.

The friends, when they began to lose their wits, supposed (not without reason) that they had been poisoned, and, sloshing with booze, decided to pass judgement on the farmer.

The best court in the world is doomed to failure when the jury is blind drunk.

"Guilty!" slurred the judge. "String him up boys!"

After they sobered up they probably felt pretty guilty about poor old Icarius, who had just been trying to be hospitable.

But thanks to the god Dionysus they now had the answer to guilt. Or at least they thought they did. They masked their sorrow in drink and called the absence of pain pleasure.

Icarius had a daughter. When her father didn't come home she was worried sick. When she found out about his death she was heartbroken.

She flung herself into a well and drowned.

Dionysus flew into a passion of rage. No one appreciated his gift like they should! How ungrateful!

He decided to pass a judgement of his own. But he too was sloshing with booze, and rather than punishing the men who killed Icarius he struck their daughters with insanity and as he laughed his drunken laugh they all hung themselves.

Dionysus had many adventures, all mad drunk. He murdered, he caused pain and suffering, he destroyed families and ruined lives.

And as those he had destroyed turned to wine, they learned to destroy too.

His followers roamed around the countryside in a state of constant intoxication, looking for mischief and generally finding it.

They say that the classical gods are a thing of the past, but I believe Dionysus still lives.

He haunts those late night bars and urges his followers, sloshing with booze, to drive themselves home.

And if you listen closely at the funeral, if you can hear past the weeping, I promise you, you will hear his drunken laugh still.

Acknowledgements

I'm jolly grateful to quite a few people over this book.

Thanks must first go to Kirsten Porteous, my classics teacher. You were such an inspiration with your warmth and friendly manner. You are a superb teacher and I shall always be deeply grateful to you.

As to you Janine Williams, thank you so very, very much for trawling through pages of original, dyslexic spelling. My unique construction of the finer points of the English language could very well bar me from the realm of writers for eternity, if it was not for good angels like yourself.

To my sister and best friend, thank you for attending to all my work for the duration of the writing of this book. I can never thank you enough for this and everything else you have ever done for me. The items on the list are simply too numerous to detail.

To Mum and Dad, who allowed me to bloom in my own leisurely time, thank you, I love you both more than words can ever say.

To Sarah Trickett, who is one of my dearest friends, and who has never shown me anything but kindness, encouragement and an unwavering belief that I can write, I love you deeply.

And finally, thanks to he who shall remain nameless, but knows who he is. The most important factor in my life. The one to whom the title 'ghastly' can never be applied. The one who is quite capable of curing his OWN headaches and does not require a subordinate to do so. To him be all the glory. Regardless of where my path in life takes me, you will always be my proudest boast.

You can follow Tiffany Rose Winters on Facebook at https://www.facebook.com/ClassicalStudiesFor Underachievers

Also, Mount Olympus seems to have suddenly become very technologically advanced, because Zeus recently got his own Facebook page. You can find him at https://www.facebook.com/ZeusSupremGod

It's a great way to keep up with the latest Ghastly Godly Gossip. Be warned though, if you write anything that is less than absolutely admiring and flattering on his wall, he will probably offer to blow you to smithereens with his thunderbolts!

Made in the USA
Columbia, SC
13 July 2019